STEVIE WONDER

Cover photo © Presselect / Alamy Stock Photo

ISBN 978-1-4950-3083-3

CORPORATION

7777 W. BLUEMOUND RD. P.O. BOX 13819 MILWAUKEE, WI 53213

Visit Hal Leonard Online at
www.halleonard.com

CONTENTS

AS

Words and Music by
STEVIE WONDER

Moderate Bossa Nova

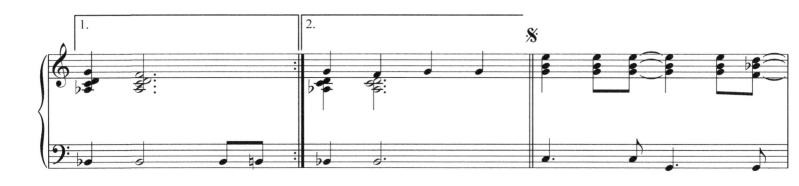

EBONY AND IVORY

Words and Music by
PAUL McCARTNEY

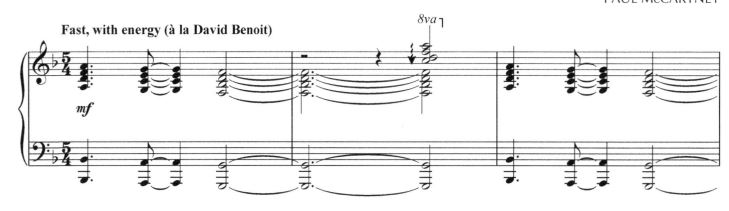

To Coda ⊕

FOR ONCE IN MY LIFE

Words by RONALD MILLER
Music by ORLANDO MURDEN

I JUST CALLED TO SAY I LOVE YOU

Words and Music by
STEVIE WONDER

22

D.S. al Coda
(with repeats)

CODA

ISN'T SHE LOVELY

Words and Music by
STEVIE WONDER

I WISH

Words and Music by
STEVIE WONDER

Easy, bluesy feel

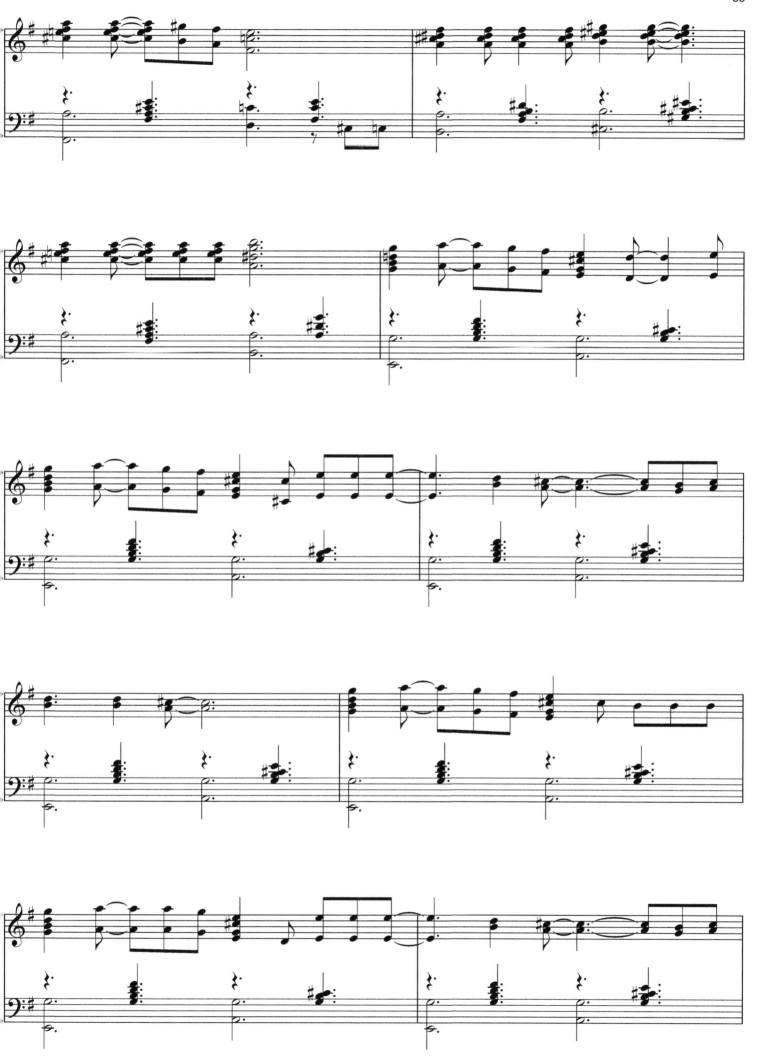

MY CHERIE AMOUR

Words and Music by STEVIE WONDER,
SYLVIA MOY and HENRY COSBY

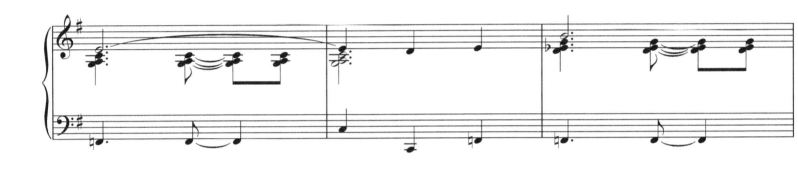

RIBBON IN THE SKY

Words and Music by
STEVIE WONDER

Jazz Ballad, slowly and freely

SIGNED, SEALED, DELIVERED I'M YOURS

Words and Music by STEVIE WONDER,
SYREETA WRIGHT, LEE GARRETT
and LULA MAE HARDAWAY

SIR DUKE

Words and Music by
STEVIE WONDER

Moderate 16th-note Shuffle

Pedal as needed

SUPERSTITION

Words and Music by
STEVIE WONDER

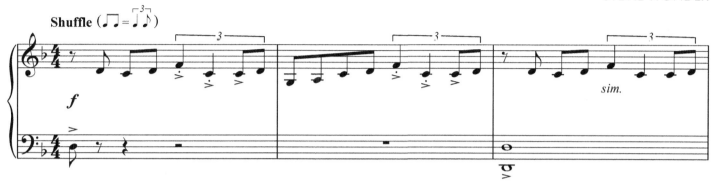

YOU ARE THE SUNSHINE OF MY LIFE

Words and Music by
STEVIE WONDER

Fast Swing

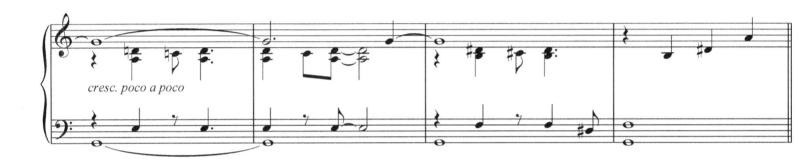

FROM HAL LEONARD

In this series, popular favorites receive unexpected fresh treatments. Uniquely reimagined and crafted for intermediate piano solo, these tunes have been All Jazzed Up!

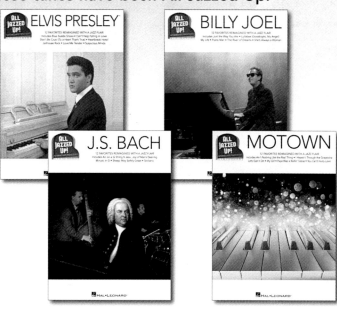

J.S. BACH
Air on the G String • Aria • Bist du bei mir (Be Thou with Me) • Gavotte • Jesu, Joy of Man's Desiring • Largo • March • Minuet in G • Musette • Sheep May Safely Graze • Siciliano • Sleepers, Awake (Wachet Auf).
00151064...$12.99

THE BEATLES
All My Loving • And I Love Her • Come Together • Eight Days a Week • Eleanor Rigby • The Fool on the Hill • Here, There and Everywhere • Lady Madonna • Lucy in the Sky with Diamonds • Michelle • While My Guitar Gently Weeps • Yesterday.
00172235...$12.99

CHRISTMAS CAROLS
Auld Lang Syne • Deck the Hall • The First Noel • Good King Wenceslas • In the Bleak Midwinter • Jingle Bells • Joy to the World • O Christmas Tree • O Come, All Ye Faithful • O Little Town of Bethlehem • Up on the Housetop • We Wish You a Merry Christmas.
00277866...$12.99

CHRISTMAS SONGS
Blue Christmas • The Christmas Song (Chestnuts Roasting on an Open Fire) • Christmas Time Is Here • Do You Hear What I Hear • Feliz Navidad • Have Yourself a Merry Little Christmas • I'll Be Home for Christmas • Merry Christmas, Darling • Silver Bells • Sleigh Ride • White Christmas • Winter Wonderland.
00236706...$12.99

COLDPLAY
Clocks • Don't Panic • Every Teardrop Is a Waterfall • Fix You • Magic • Paradise • The Scientist • A Sky Full of Stars • Speed of Sound • Trouble • Viva La Vida • Yellow.
00149026...$12.99

DISNEY
Belle • Circle of Life • Cruella De Vil • Ev'rybody Wants to Be a Cat • It's a Small World • Let It Go • Mickey Mouse March • Once upon a Dream • Part of Your World • Supercalifragilisticexpialidocious • Under the Sea • When She Loved Me.
00151072...$14.99

JIMI HENDRIX
Castles Made of Sand • Crosstown Traffic • Fire • Foxey Lady • Hey Joe • Little Wing • Manic Depression • Purple Haze • Spanish Castle Magic • The Wind Cries Mary.
00174441...$12.99

BILLY JOEL
And So It Goes • Honesty • It's Still Rock and Roll to Me • Just the Way You Are • The Longest Time • Lullabye (Goodnight, My Angel) • My Life • New York State of Mind • Piano Man • The River of Dreams • She's Always a Woman • She's Got a Way.
00149039...$12.99

MOTOWN
Ain't Nothing like the Real Thing • How Sweet It Is (To Be Loved by You) • I Can't Help Myself (Sugar Pie, Honey Bunch) • I Heard It Through the Grapevine • I Want You Back • Let's Get It On • My Girl • Never Can Say Goodbye • Overjoyed • Papa Was a Rollin' Stone • Still • You Can't Hurry Love.
00174482...$12.99

NIRVANA
About a Girl • All Apologies • Come as You Are • Dumb • Heart Shaped Box • In Bloom • Lithium • The Man Who Sold the World • On a Plain • (New Wave) Polly • Rape Me • Smells like Teen Spirit.
00149025...$12.99

OZZY OSBOURNE
Crazy Train • Dreamer • Flying High Again • Goodbye to Romance • Iron Man • Mama, I'm Coming Home • Mr. Crowley • No More Tears • Over the Mountain • Paranoid • Perry Mason • Time After Time.
00149040...$12.99

ELVIS PRESLEY
Blue Suede Shoes • Can't Help Falling in Love • Cryin' in the Chapel • Don't • Don't Be Cruel (To a Heart That's True) • Heartbreak Hotel • I Want You, I Need You, I Love You • Jailhouse Rock • Love Me Tender • Suspicious Minds • The Wonder of You • You Don't Have to Say You Love Me.
00198895...$12.99

STEVIE WONDER
As • Ebony and Ivory • For Once in My Life • I Just Called to Say I Love You • I Wish • Isn't She Lovely • My Cherie Amour • Ribbon in the Sky • Signed, Sealed, Delivered I'm Yours • Sir Duke • Superstition • You Are the Sunshine of My Life.
00149090...$12.99

www.halleonard.com

Prices, contents and availability subject to change without notice.

Disney characters and artwork © Disney Enterprises, Inc.

0618

jazz piano solos series

Each volume features exciting new arrangements with chord symbols of the songs which helped define a style.

jazz blues

bill evans

christmas songs

pop standards

christmas standards

big band era

vol. 1 miles davis
00306521......................$19.99

vol. 2 jazz blues
00306522......................$19.99

vol. 3 latin jazz
00310621......................$19.99

vol. 4 bebop jazz
00310709......................$19.99

vol. 5 cool jazz
00310710......................$17.99

vol. 6 hard bop
00323507......................$16.99

vol. 7 smooth jazz
00310727......................$19.99

vol. 8 jazz pop
00311786......................$19.99

vol. 9 duke ellington
00311787......................$19.99

vol. 10 jazz ballads
00311788......................$19.99

vol. 11 soul jazz
00311789......................$17.99

vol. 12 swinging jazz
00311797......................$19.99

vol. 13 jazz gems
00311899......................$17.99

vol. 14 jazz classics
00311900......................$19.99

vol. 15 bossa nova
00311906......................$17.99

vol. 16 disney
00312121......................$19.99

vol. 17 antonio carlos jobim
00312122......................$19.99

vol. 18 modern jazz quartet
00307270......................$16.99

vol. 19 bill evans
00307273......................$19.99

vol. 20 gypsy jazz
00307289......................$19.99

vol. 21 new orleans
00312169......................$17.99

vol. 22 classic jazz
00001529......................$17.99

vol. 23 jazz for lovers
00312548......................$19.99

vol. 24 john coltrane
00307395......................$19.99

vol. 25 christmas songs
00101790......................$17.99

vol. 26 george gershwin
00103353......................$19.99

vol. 27 late night jazz
00312547......................$19.99

vol. 28 the beatles
00119302......................$19.99

vol. 29 elton john
00120968......................$19.99

vol. 30 cole porter
00123364......................$19.99

vol. 31 cocktail piano
00123366......................$19.99

vol. 32 johnny mercer
00123367......................$16.99

vol. 33 gospel
00127079......................$19.99

vol. 34 horace silver
00139633......................$16.99

vol. 35 stride piano
00139685......................$17.99

vol. 36 broadway jazz
00144365......................$19.99

vol. 37 silver screen jazz
00144366......................$17.99

vol. 38 henry mancini
00146382......................$19.99

vol. 39 sacred christmas carols
00147678......................$17.99

vol. 40 charlie parker
00149089......................$16.99

vol. 41 pop standards
00153656......................$17.99

vol. 42 dave brubeck
00154634......................$17.99

vol. 43 candlelight jazz
00154901......................$17.99

vol. 44 jazz standards
00160856......................$19.99

vol. 45 christmas standards
00172024......................$19.99

vol. 46 cocktail jazz
00172025......................$19.99

vol. 47 hymns
00172026......................$17.99

vol. 48 blue skies & other irving berlin songs
00197873......................$19.99

vol. 49 thelonious monk
00232767......................$16.99

vol. 50 best smooth jazz
00233277......................$16.99

vol. 51 disney favorites
00233315......................$19.99

vol. 52 bebop classics
00234075......................$16.99

vol. 53 jazz-rock
00256715......................$16.99

vol. 54 jazz fusion
00256716......................$16.99

vol. 55 ragtime
00274961......................$16.99

vol. 56 pop ballads
00274962......................$16.99

vol. 57 pat metheny
00277058......................$19.99

vol. 58 big band era
00284837......................$17.99

vol. 59 west coast jazz
00290792......................$17.99

vol. 60 boogie woogie
00363280......................$17.99

vol. 61 christmas classics
00367872......................$17.99

vol. 62 coffee table jazz
00379205......................$19.99

vol. 63 classical jazz
00428375......................$19.99

jazz ballads

george gershwin

late night jazz

hymns

HAL•LEONARD®

Visit Hal Leonard Online at
www.halleonard.com

Prices, contents & availability subject to change without notice.